COLLEGIATECOOK.COM'S
USF GAMEDAY RECIPES

CELEBRATE THE BULLS' NEXT "W" WITH 50+ SNACKS, TREATS & DRINKS

Collegiate Cookbook: USF Gameday Edition

Copyright © 2014 by Candace and Nathan Davison

Cover by: Nathan Davison

ISBN-13: 9781500794279
ISBN-10: 1500794279

Collegiate Cook
www.collegiatecook.com
Email: Candace@collegiatecook.com

Follow Collegiate Cook on Twitter:
@collegiatecook

Printed in U.S.A

ARE YOU READY FOR SOME FOOD...AND FOOTBALL?

Gameday has a sort of frenetic energy that pulses through you the moment you catch a glimpse of the stadium. Maybe it's the fact that there are grown men covered in glitter and body paint. Maybe it's the feeling that all those players, suited up, represent you, your college, your ambitions. Maybe it's the magnetic thrill of feeling like you belong to something bigger than just you.

Whatever the feeling is, it's worth celebrating with more than the same ol' cardboard-crust pizza you eat every Friday night.

Your tastebuds deserve more than that.

That's why this cookbook was born. We want to make every gameday feel like the Event of the Week, whether you're watching from the student section or on a grainy TV 1,200 miles away.

Each game of the USF football season inspired at least one recipe, and several more came from my family and friends' favorite dishes to share at watch parties, tailgates and get-togethers. Some took several iterations to get right (waffle-battered chicken tenders, we're lookin' at you), whereas others were such classics that we could prepare them while fully engrossed in SportsCenter. What excites us the most, though, is that this cookbook isn't just an opportunity to share a few I-want-to-eat-my-body-weight-in-this dishes — it's a chance to give back: **25 percent of the proceeds from each copy sold are being donated to Honors College scholarships.** We wouldn't be able to get our degree without the generosity of others, which is why we're so grateful that you're helping us pay it forward. (Thank you, thank you, THANK YOU for making this possible!)

—Candace & Nathan Davison

P.S. — Check the index (pages 113-115) to see all of the places each ingredient is used.

FIND MORE RECIPES & TAILGATE IDEAS AT COLLEGIATECOOK.COM

TABLE OF CONTENTS

SAVORY SNACKS, CONTINUED

SWEETS

A SIGNATURE DISH FOR EVERY GAME:

USF-Themed:
- "Sweet Victory" Green Velvet Cupcakes
- Rocky's Unstoppable Snack Mix
- "That's BS!" Cookies
- Green & Gold Vegetable Fritters
- The Raging Bulls Mojitos
- Fourth-Quarter Kaboom Cookies

What to Serve When We're Playing...
- **Western Carolina University:** Baked Sweet Potato Fries
- **East Carolina University:** Pirates' Cinnamon Sangria
  Tulane: Shrimp Po'Boy Sliders
- **University of Cincinnati:** Red & Black Italian Pasta Salad
- **UConn:** Honey-Blueberry Overnight Oats
- **University of Wisconsin:** Macaroni & Cheese Pizza Bites
- **Notre Dame:** Fightin' Irish Mini Shepherd's Pies
- **University of Houston:** Houston, Texas Margaritas
- **University of Memphis:** Pulled Pork Sliders
- **Southern Methodist University:** "We'll Mess with Texas" Blueberry Lemonade
- **McNeese State:** Chocolate-Hazelnut Cowboy Cookies
- **University of Central Florida:** Fruit Kabobs with Honey Caramel Sauce
- **University of Florida:** "Better Than Gator Tail" Waffle-Battered Chicken Tenders
- **University of Miami:** Sweet & Sour Meatball Sliders

TWEET OR INSTAGRAM YOUR GAMEDAY PHOTOS USING #HOWBULLSTAILGATE & WE'LL FEATURE 'EM ON COLLEGIATECOOK.COM!

BRUNCH RECIPES

Noon games mean the party starts early. We've got the tastiest wake-up calls to fuel you up.

PEANUT BUTTER BANANA PANCAKES, PAGE 18

A SOUTHERN-FRIED CLASSIC:
WAFFLE-BATTERED CHICKEN TENDERS

SERVES 5-6

TIME COMMITMENT:
1-2 HOURS TO MARINATE
30-40 MINUTES TO COOK

INGREDIENTS:

2-3 boneless chicken breasts, cut into strips

¾ cup buttermilk

1 tablespoon tarragon

1 tablespoon thyme

½ teaspoon cayenne pepper

¾ cup flour

½ teaspoon garlic powder

½ teaspoon onion powder

2 cups vegetable oil

Belgian waffle mix (plus any necessary ingredients to prepare batter)

Mini toaster waffles (optional)

Maple syrup, for serving

STEPS:

1. Place the chicken tenders in a large, resealable bowl and cover with buttermilk, tarragon, thyme and cayenne pepper. Mix it up. Cover, stick in a refrigerator and let it marinate for at least an hour (you can leave it overnight if you want; the longer the chicken marinates, the more batter it will hold).

2. When you're ready to cook the chicken, pour the oil into a frying pan and set it to medium-high heat. Let it heat to 350° F. As it heats, mix the flour, garlic and onion powder in a shallow bowl. In a second shallow bowl, prepare the waffle batter.

3. Take each piece of buttermilk-coated chicken and dredge it in the flour mixture. Using tongs, gently lower each strip in the oil. (Watch out for splatters!) Cook for 2 minutes, flip and cook 2 minutes more.

4. As each tender is finished cooking, place on a plate lined with paper towels. Once all of the tenders are fried, dip them in the waffle batter and fry them a second time, for about 2 minutes on each side. Let them cool for 10-12 minutes before serving. When you cut the chicken, make sure it's all white inside.

Optional: Cut the tenders into slices and serve atop mini toaster waffles (toasted, of course), with maple syrup on the side for dipping.

SATURDAY MORNING PARFAIT SHOOTERS

SERVES: 4 * TIME COMMITMENT: 5 MINUTES

In case you were wondering what your morning tailgates were missing, we've got two words: yogurt bar. Just grab a table, create a buffet line of your favorite toppings and watch as the hordes of hungry fans descend. Because sometimes, a drive-thru egg sammie just doesn't cut it.

COMBINATIONS WE LOVE:

- **Fourth-Quarter Fuel:** Cheerios with bananas and strawberry yogurt

- **Bellini Breakfast:** Kashi Go Lean with peaches and peach yogurt

- **No Time for French Toast:** Cinnamon Toast Crunch with blueberries and vanilla yogurt

- **The Benchwarmer:** Shredded wheat with raspberries, mini chocolate chips and vanilla yogurt

- **Pseudo-Pina Colada:** Shredded wheat with shredded coconut, pineapple chunks (drain the juice beforehand) and vanilla yogurt

- **12th Man's Reward:** Corn flakes with cherries (remove pits first!), mini semisweet chocolate chips and cherry yogurt

- **Thrown for a Loop:** Froot Loops with bananas and vanilla yogurt

- **Almost-PB&J:** Reese's Puffs, strawberries and vanilla yogurt, swirled with a tablespoon of melted peanut butter

HONEY-BLUEBERRY OVERNIGHT OATS

If you're thinking of heading to an away game -- particularly one 1,000-plus miles away, like when USF plays UConn in Storrs, CT -- you'll need fuel for the haul. This make-ahead dish takes seconds to prepare, so you can grab it and go on your way to cheer on those B-U-L-L-S.

SERVES: 4   TIME COMMITMENT: 3-5 MINUTES

INGREDIENTS:

2 cups rolled oats

2 cups skim milk

2 (5.3- to 6-ounce) containers of low-fat Greek yogurt

2 tablespoons honey

2/3 cup blueberries

2 tablespoons ground flax seed (optional)

STEPS:

1. Combine all ingredients in a bowl, stirring until all oats are submerged.

2. Cover with plastic wrap (or lid, if it's a resealable bowl) and refrigerate overnight. If you don't have that long, keep it in the fridge for at least an hour to let the oats soften.

USF TRIVIA: THE BULLS HAVE PLAYED FIVE GAMES IN UNDER-40-DEGREE WEATHER (TWO OF WHICH WERE AGAINST UCONN). WHAT WAS THE MOST FRIGID TEMPERATURE AS OF 2012? (A) 19 DEGREES, (B) 24 DEGREES, (C) 29 DEGREES OR (D) 32 DEGREES

(The answer is on the last page.)

CHEESY BACON TATER FRITTATA

SERVES: 6-8   TIME COMMITMENT: 30-35 MINUTES

INGREDIENTS:

4-5 slices turkey bacon (or regular bacon)

1 cup frozen tater tots

6 eggs

2 tablespoons water

1 handful shredded cheese (we recommend colby jack or sharp cheddar)

Salsa (optional)

STEPS:

1. Preheat the oven to 425° F. As it heats, cook turkey bacon over medium heat in a frying pan until crispy. Place bacon on a plate lined with paper towels to absorb excess grease. Turn off the burner.

2. Arrange the tots in a single layer on the bottom of the 8-inch or 9-inch round cake pan. Once the bacon has cooled, crumble it on top.

3. In a small bowl, crack the eggs, add the water, and stir vigorously until thoroughly combined. Pour on top of the tots and bacon in the cake pan.

4. Sprinkle cheese on top, then place in the oven and cook for 22-25 minutes, or until the eggs have solidified and the top of the frittata is lightly browned.

5. Let it cool a few minutes, then serve with a dollop of salsa, if you're feeling adventurous.

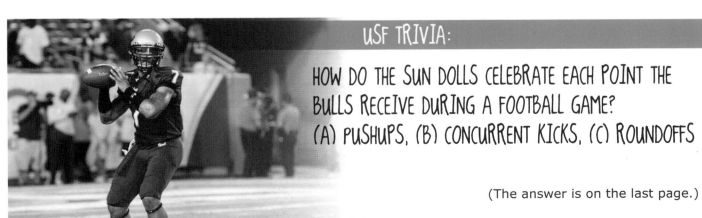

USF TRIVIA:

HOW DO THE SUN DOLLS CELEBRATE EACH POINT THE BULLS RECEIVE DURING A FOOTBALL GAME?
(A) PUSHUPS, (B) CONCURRENT KICKS, (C) ROUNDOFFS

(The answer is on the last page.)

UNFORGETTABULL BACON PUMPKIN PANCAKES

Nothing says fall quite like Saturday morning football -- and pumpkin-flavored anything. Capture the best of both worlds by serving these savory-sweet, bacon-studded beauties at the next noon game.

SERVES: 4-5   TIME COMMITMENT: 20-25 MINUTES

INGREDIENTS:

4-5 strips of bacon

1 1/2 cups milk

1 cup pumpkin puree (AKA canned pumpkin)

1 egg

2 tablespoons vegetable oil

1 teaspoon vanilla extract

2 cups flour

3 tablespoons brown sugar

2 teaspoons baking powder

1 teaspoon baking soda

2 teaspoons cinnamon

1/2 teaspoon salt

STEPS:

1. Chop bacon, then cook it over medium heat in a frying pan until the fat is no longer translucent. Drain the grease and transfer the bacon pieces to a plate lined with paper towels.

2. Mix the milk, pumpkin, egg, oil and vanilla in a small bowl. In a large bowl, combine the flour, brown sugar, baking soda, baking powder, cinnamon and salt. Fold in the pumpkin mixture, stirring it just enough so that all ingredients are combined. (The more you mix, the less fluffy the pancakes will be.)

3. With the burner on medium heat, pour 1/4 cup pumpkin batter onto the frying pan. Sprinkle some bacon pieces on top, and flip the pancake once its edges have rounded and the bubbling has begun to slow down.

Tip: If you're hosting a watch party and want to serve all of the pancakes at once, preheat the oven to 200° F and keep all of your freshly flipped treats there until you're ready to eat. It will keep the pancakes warm without drying them out.

PEANUT BUTTER BANANA PANCAKES

Optional, but highly encouraged: Lightly smear extra peanut butter between each pancake. The pancakes' heat will cause the peanut butter to melt, resulting in rich, velvety bliss. Drizzle with maple syrup.

SERVES: 4-5   TIME COMMITMENT: 15-18 MINUTES

INGREDIENTS:

1 1/4 cups flour

1/2 cup rolled oats

3 1/2 teaspoons baking powder

1 teaspoon salt

1 tablespoon white sugar

1 1/4 cups milk

1 egg

2 tablespoons butter

3 tablespoons peanut butter

1 banana, sliced

STEPS:

1. Stir the flour, baking soda, rolled oats and sugar in a large bowl.

2. Place the butter and peanut butter in a microwave-safe bowl. Heat it in the microwave for 20-second intervals, stirring in between, until everything has melted completely.

3. Pour the melted butters into the bowl o' dry ingredients. Mix it in, and as you stir, add in the egg and milk.

4. Let a frying pan heat over the grill (or burner on medium) for a few minutes. Pour a palm-sized amount of batter onto the pan. Top it with a few slices of banana, and once small bubbles form in the batter, flip it to the other side. When both sides are lightly golden, move the pancake to a plate and start another.

TAILGATERS: PREP BATTER THE NIGHT BEFORE. STORE IT IN A PLASTIC RESEALABLE CONTAINER IN AN ICE-FILLED COOLER. COOK ON GRILL USING FRYING PAN.

"WE'LL MESS WITH TEX-
AS" BLUEBERRY LEMON-
ADE, PAGE 24

COCKTAILS

WHEN THAT RED PLASTIC CUP OF LUKEWARM
BEER JUST WON'T CUT IT

THE RAGING BULLS MOJITO

We've found your official gameday drink. It's refreshing, it's light, but like the Bulls, you better not underestimate it: This mojito packs a punch.

SERVES 1*

TIME COMMITMENT: 5 MINUTES PREP

INGREDIENTS:

1 teaspoon sugar

8 mint leaves, torn

1 ounce light rum

½ ounce lime juice

6 ounces Fresca
(or other lemon-lime soda)

Ice

STEPS::

1. Combine sugar, mint leaves, rum and lime juice in a cocktail shaker or lidded bottle (tighten cap after pouring in ingredients).

2. Give it 4-5 good shakes, pour over ice. Top with Fresca.

* THIS RECIPE CAN BE EASILY DOUBLED, TRIPLED OR QUADRUPLED. WE'RE JUST SHOWING YOU THE INGREDIENTS FOR ONE SO YOU DON'T OVERWHELM YOUR COCKTAIL SHAKER (OR LIDDED JAR).

"WE'LL MESS WITH TEXAS" BLUEBERRY LEMONADE

SERVES 5

TIME COMMITMENT: 5 MINUTES PREP
(PLUS OPTIONAL VODKA INFUSING; SEE NOTE BELOW)

INGREDIENTS:

1 pint blueberries, rinsed

1 lemon, sliced into thin coins

½ gallon premade lemonade

5 ounces vodka (optional)

In honor of the SMU Mustangs' colors, we dreamed up a sweet-yet-tart blueberry lemonade. It's just the rejuvenating boost you need to rally after halftime. (Oh, and did we mention it's so easy it barely qualifies as a recipe?)

STEPS:

1. For the blueberry ice cubes: Place 1-2 blueberries in each compartment of an ice cube tray. Fill with water and freeze.

2. For the drink: Muddle 1 tablespoon blueberries in the bottom of each cocktail glass (Muddle = Getting out your aggression by smashing the blueberries with a spoon). Add in a few lemon slices. Top with lemonade and vodka, stir everything to combine. Serve with a lemon slice on the rim.

Take things one step further: For a truly infused drink, create blueberry-infused vodka: One day before the big game, combine the blueberries and vodka in a mason jar. Let them steep overnight. Remove the blueberries and muddle as the recipe suggests, then add in the blueberry-tinted vodka to the drink. (The drink will have a bright purple tint.)

PLUNDERED FROM THE PIRATES: CINNAMON SANGRIA

This cinnamon-spiced sangria embodies all the flavors of fall, making it the perfect drink to serve on a crisp gameday against the East Carolina Pirates. Even if you're not hitting up the Bulls-Pirates game, keep this recipe on hand anytime the temperature dips below 75.

TIME COMMITMENT: 5-7 MINUTES PREP, 2-3 HOURS TO CHILL

INGREDIENTS:

2 tablespoons sugar

1 teaspoon cinnamon

½ cup brandy

2 apples, cubed

1 bottle dry red wine (like Rioja)

1 cup sparkling water (or club soda)

STEPS:

1. Mix the cinnamon, sugar, brandy and apples in a large pitcher or carafe, letting the sugar dissolve. Top with the bottle of wine and place it in the fridge to chill for at least 2 hours.

2. Before serving, add in the sparkling water.

USF TRIVIA: WHAT'S THE NAME OF USF'S FIRST PRESIDENT?

(The answer is on the last page.)

HOUSTON, TEXAS MARGARITAS

Need a drink for a crowd? Well, this is it. The limeade and beer stretch these 'ritas farther than the traditional kind, and for a fraction of the price. Serve this drink the next time the Bulls face the Houston Cougars.

SERVES 6-8 * TIME COMMITMENT: 5 MINUTES

INGREDIENTS:

1 two-liter bottle of lemon-lime soda
1 12-ounce container of frozen limeade
6 ounces tequila
1 bottle of Corona

STEPS:

Mix all ingredients together and serve over crushed ice. Salted rim and lime slice optional, though highly encouraged.

WATERMELON MARGARITAS

SERVES 6-8 * TIME COMMITMENT: 10 MINUTES

INGREDIENTS:

5 cups cubed, seedless watermelon
2 tablespoons sugar
2 limes, juiced
2 cups ice
7 ounces Triple Sec
9 ounces tequila

STEPS:

Puree the watermelon, sugar, ice and Triple Sec in a blender.
Once it's reached a smoothie-like consistency, pour it into a pitcher and stir in the lime juice and tequila.

Tip: The hollowed-out watermelon makes for an awesome serving bowl.

28

THE MORNING-GAME MIMOSA

The secret to a great mimosa: Don't stir. Pour the Champagne first, and the carbonation will naturally mix things up.

SERVES 1
TIME COMMITMENT: 2 MINUTES

INGREDIENTS:

4 ounces Champagne (or sparkling white wine)

4 ounces orange juice

STEPS:

Pour the Champagne into a glass, then top with orange juice. Serve immediately, before the drink can lose its fizz.

SWEET & SOUR MEATBALL
SLIDERS, PAGES 52-53

SAVORY SNACKS

DISHES SO INCREDIBLE YOU'LL DROOL ALL OVER YOURSELF JUST THINKING ABOUT 'EM (DON'T FORGET TO TWEET YOUR CREATIONS: #HOWBULLSTAILGATE)

MEMPHIS TIGERS PULLED PORK SLIDERS

The South is known for barbecue, so it's only fitting that a rumble between two such teams would involve a heaping helping of piggalicious comfort food. (Yes, you read correctly.) The best part? The slow cooker does most of the work, so it's like your meal is catered. We'll mark that as a "W" any day of the week.

BY NATHAN DAVISON, SEAN ARGO & MICHAEL WASSERMAN

* SERVES 6-8 * TIME COMMITMENT: 10 MINUTES TO PREP, 6+ HOURS COOKING

INGREDIENTS:

1 vidalia onion

3 lbs pork shoulder, boneless

1 can Ro-Tel tomatoes (as spicy as you like it)

1 packet onion soup mix (Lipton works quite well)

32 ounces low sodium beef broth

4 tablespoons Liquid Smoke

1 bottle your fave bbq sauce

1 tube premade biscuit dough

STEPS:

1. Chop onion into thick slices and line the bottom of a large slow cooker.

2. Stab pork 10-15 times with a fork, then massage liquid smoke into the punctures and throughout the surface of the shoulder.

3. Rub 1/2 of the packet of onion soup mix onto the pork. Place the pork in slow cooker on top of the onion.

4. Add the can of tomatoes, the beef broth and remaining onion soup mix to the slow cooker.

5. Put the lid on the slow cooker, crank the heat up to high, and wait...for six hours! (Trust us, it'll be worth it!)

6. Once it's ready, drain out the excess juices, then use two forks to shred the pork.

7. Add generous amounts of your favorite sauce, and stir thoroughly.

8. Prepare biscuits according to the package instructions, then slice and serve with pulled pork.

BLACK BEAN AND CORN SALSA

RECIPE COURTESY OF KRISTIN ARNOLD RUYLE   *   SERVES 8   *   TIME COMMITMENT: 15 MINUTES

This recipe makes a mixing bowl full of salsa, and for good reason: After one bite, you'll want to grab a spoon and down it like soup. Huge thanks to USF Mass Communications instructor Kristin Arnold Ruyle for introducing us to it. We'll never be the same, and you won't, either.

INGREDIENTS:

2 cans black beans
2 cans yellow corn
½ sweet onion
1 avocado
2 tomatoes
1 lime
2 tablespoons cilantro, chopped
olive oil
vinegar
salt and pepper

STEPS:

1. Drain excess juices from the cans of black beans and corn, and pour them into a large bowl.
2. Finely chop the onion, avocado and tomato. Add them into the bowl, along with the juice from the lime and the remaining ingredients. Season with salt and pepper to taste.

USF TRIVIA: WHO DID THE BULLS PLAY IN THEIR FIRST BASKETBALL GAME? (BONUS: WHO WON?)

(The answer is on the last page.)

MAC & CHEESE PIZZA BITES

SERVES: 8   *   TIME COMMITMENT: 25-30 MINUTES

In 2014, the Bulls face off against the Wisconsin Badgers for the very first time, and in honor of that matchup in the Midwest, we thought we'd prepare our own twist on one of the most famous dishes in the area: Mac & Cheese Pizza. If you're tailgating in Madison, you have to visit Ian's Pizza to try a slice. If you're hosting a watch party, treat yourself to these bad boys.

INGREDIENTS:

1 package macaroni & cheese

1 bag mini bagels (at least 4)

1 jar alfredo sauce

1 cup shredded sharp cheddar

Pepper, to taste

STEPS:

1. Cook the macaroni and cheese according to the package's instructions. Set aside.

2. Turn the oven to broil and halve the bagels. Place them halved-side up on a baking sheet and broil for 3-4 minutes, or until lightly browned.

3. Remove from oven. Lightly slather the tops of the bagels with alfredo sauce (like you would cream cheese). Top with macaroni and cheese, then sprinkle with shredded cheddar. Place in the oven for about 30 seconds, or until the cheese has melted.

4. Sprinkle with pepper, if you choose.

MARK YOUR CALENDARS: USF PLAYS WISCONSIN ON SEPT. 27, 2014, AND AGAIN ON SEPT. 16, 2017.

SPICY GREEN BEAN "FRIES"

Tailgate foods tend to fall into two categories: greasy and/or deep-fried. While both are delicious, too many can feel like a bowling ball in your stomach. This appetizer bucks the trend; it's oven-baked, oil-free and yet it's still loaded with flavor. Go easy on the cayenne; you can always sprinkle more on later.

SERVES: 4-5 ＊ TIME COMMITMENT: 20-22 MINUTES

INGREDIENTS:

2 packages frozen green beans

1/2 cup shredded parmesan cheese

2 teaspoons cayenne pepper

1 tablespoon garlic powder

STEPS:

1. Preheat the oven to 450° F.
2. Heat green beans in the microwave for 4 minutes, until fully thawed. Drain any excess liquids, and place in a single layer on a parchment-lined baking sheet.
3. Sprinkle with parmesan cheese, cayenne pepper and garlic powder.
4. Cook in the oven for 18-20 minutes, or until desired crispness. (If the green beans are still a little mushy, you can broil them for 30-45 seconds.)

USF TRIVIA: USF'S MARCHING BAND, THE HERD OF THUNDER, DEBUTED IN WHAT YEAR?

(The answer is on the last page.)

2 WAYS TO LIVEN UP DEVILED EGGS

SERVINGS: YIELDS 2 DOZEN EGGS   *   TIME COMMITMENT: 15-20 MINUTES TO PREPARE, 20 MINUTES TO COOL

FOR THE EGGS:

You'll need: 1 dozen large eggs, water
1. Place the eggs in a large saucepan and cover with water. Heat to medium-high on the stovetop, and once the water comes to a rolling boil, remove the saucepan from the heat and turn off the burner.
2. Give the eggs 20 minutes to cool, then drain the water from the pot and peel the eggs. Halve them, removing the yolks and collecting them in a mixing bowl. Now you're ready to create the filling:

CHIPOTLE-BACON STYLE:

Yolks
6 tablespoons mayonnaise
1 tablespoon chili powder
2 tablespoons Worstershire sauce
1 tablespoons garlic powder
6 strips cooked bacon, crumbled

Smash the cooked yolks into small pieces and blend with the mayo, chili powder, Worstershire and garlic powder. Fill in egg halves and top with crumbled bacon.

GARLIC-HERB STYLE:

Yolks
6 tablespoons mayonnaise
2 tablespoons garlic powder
1 tablespoon thyme
1 tablespoon dried basil (or Italian seasoning)

Smash the yolks into small pieces and blend with the mayo, garlic powder, thyme and basil. Fill in egg white halves and sprinkle a little extra basil or Italian seasoning on top for garnish.

41

NACHO-CRUSTED CHICKEN SLIDERS

SERVES: 4-5 ✳ TIME COMMITMENT: 35-40 MINUTES

Anybody can do fried chicken sliders, but you? You're taking it to the next level. These chicken tenders are breaded in Cool Ranch Doritos and baked, so they have all the zesty kick without the grease. For spicer chicken, marinate the tenderloins in Buffalo sauce instead of salad dressing.

INGREDIENTS:

1 pound boneless, skinless chicken tenderloins

1 bottle salad dressing (to marinate; Italian, Honey Balsamic or Ranch are great)

2 cups flour

1 teaspoon cayenne pepper

1/2 teaspoon pepper

3 eggs

1 bag flavored tortilla chips (we like Doritos)

1 package slider buns

1 head Bibb lettuce

1 bottle Ranch dressing

STEPS:

1. Halve the chicken tenderloins and place them in a gallon-sized resealable bag and coat with salad dressing. Let it marinate for 30 minutes or longer.
1. Preheat the oven to 350° F.
2. As the oven heats, set up three bowls for breading the chicken. Fill the first bowl with a mixture of flour, cayenne pepper and black pepper. Crack eggs into the second bowl and whisk them together to create an egg wash. Smash Doritos and place them in the third bowl.
3. Dip each piece of chicken in the flour mixture, then the egg wash, then the crumbled Doritos. (You may need to sprinkle more chips on top to thoroughly coat each piece.) Place each breaded piece of chicken on a parchment-lined baking sheet.
4. Bake chicken in the oven for 27-30 minutes, or until fully cooked. (There should be no pink showing when you cut 'em in half.)
5. Assemble the sliders: Cut each bun in half. Place a piece of lettuc on the bottom bun, then the chicken, then drizzle with ranch and top with the other half of the bun. Boom!

LOADED BAKED POTATO SALAD

SERVES 8-10 * TIME COMMITMENT: 25-27 MINUTES

Even people who *detest* potato salad will fall for this cheesy, chivey, bacon-studded take on the classic tailgating side. Feel free to mix in any of your favorite baked potato toppings: finely chopped broccoli, onions or sautéed peppers, blue cheese crumbles — you name it.

INGREDIENTS:

7-8 large Russet or Yukon Gold potatoes
1/2 cup mayonnaise
1 cup sour cream
2 teaspoons garlic powder (optional)
9 strips bacon, cooked and crumbled
2/3 cup shredded sharp cheddar cheese
1/3 cup chopped chives

STEPS:

1. Wash and cut the potatoes into 1-inch pieces and place in a large saucepan. Cover with water and bring the pot to a boil. Cook for 15-17 minutes, stirring every few minutes. Drain water.
2. In a separate bowl, mix mayo, sour cream and garlic powder. Add in potatoes and toss until thoroughly combined.
3. Fold in the bacon, cheese and chives. Serve cool or at room temperature, and try to stay modest when you're overcome by rave reviews.

ANTI-FRESHMAN 15 TIP:

Substitute plain Greek yogurt for the mayo and sour cream. It tastes the same, but packs more protein!

USF TRIVIA: THE BULLS WERE ALMOST THE... (A) DESERT RATS, (B) FROGS OR (C) WILD CHICKENS?

(The answer is on the last page.)

BAKED PULLED PORK WONTONS

SERVES: 8 * TIME COMMITMENT: 30 MINUTES

When you're making a batch of pulled pork in a slow cooker, you might as well make the biggest batch possible, and enjoy it as many ways as possible. Topping nachos, as sliders on biscuits (a la page 33), but especially -- and most unexpectedly -- as wontons.

INGREDIENTS:

½ pound cooked pulled pork (Follow the recipe on page 33 or buy premade)

½ jar BBQ sauce

1 package wonton wrappers

1 bunch scallions

½ cup water

Olive oil (optional)

STEPS:

1. Preheat oven to 350° F. Mix drained pulled pork with with as much BBQ sauce as you see fit. Add one teaspoon of the mixture to one corner of each wonton wrapper.

2. Finely dice scallions and sprinkle a few on each mound of pulled pork.

3. Dip your finger into the water and use it to wet the two edges of the wrapper closest to the pulled pork. Fold the wrapper in half, so it covers the pulled pork. Use your fingers to seal it, removing any air bubbles. (It should look like a triangle.)

4. Fold over the two farthest corners of the wrapper, so it forms a small crown, and lightly brush the top of each wonton with olive oil. Place each completed wonton on a baking sheet.

5. Cook wontons for 10-12 minutes, or until lightly browned. Let cool for a few minutes, so they're warm but not hot, and serve with low-sodium soy sauce for dipping.

EXTRA WONTON WRAPPERS? PUT 'EM TO USE WITH THE RECIPE ON PAGE 56.

OR MAKE BUFFALO CHICKEN DIP:
SKIP THE CRESCENT ROLLS AND HEAT THE FILLING IN
THE OVEN FOR 10-12 MINUTES. SERVE WITH CHIPS.

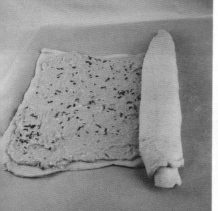
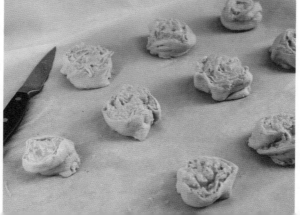

BUFFALO "WE AIN'T CHICKEN!" PINWHEELS

Anybody can bring hot wings to a game. But you, my friend, can bring the game changer. My childhood bestie, Nicole, makes an out-of-this-world Buffalo Chicken Dip, which inspired this savory pastry. This cheesy appetizer is perfect for a faceoff against the Wisconsin Badgers.

SERVES 8-10 (2 EACH) * TIME COMMITMENT: 10 MINUTES PREP, 11-13 MINUTES TO COOK

INGREDIENTS:

8-ounce package of cream cheese, softened

1/2 cup ranch dressing

1/2 cup buffalo sauce (or hot sauce)

1/3 cup sharp cheddar cheese

28-ounce can of shredded chicken breasts, drained (or 2 homecooked shredded chicken breasts*)

2 tubes of Crescent Rolls

STEPS:

1. Preheat the oven to 375° F. In a mixing bowl, combine the cream cheese, ranch and buffalo sauce until all large lumps are gone. Stir in the shredded cheese and chicken.

2. Unroll a tube of Crescent Rolls so that the dough forms a large rectangle. (Do not tear it into triangles, no matter how tempting those perforated edges are!) Slather the buffalo sauce over all the dough, then roll it up into a long log. Use a knife to cut it into ½-inch-thick coins.

   Tip: Is the dough flattening as you try to cut it? Stick it in the freezer for 5 minutes for easier cutting. (Also, you can easily reshape mushy pinwheels into more circular shapes, so don't worry about it.)

3. Place each pinwheel about 2 inches apart on the baking sheet. Cook for 11-13 minutes, or until the dough is lightly golden. Let 'em cool for 8-10 minutes before serving.

*Make your own shredded chicken: Place 2 boneless, skinless chicken breasts in a slow cooker and cover with low-sodium chicken broth, 2 tablespoons garlic powder, 1 cup water. Cook on high for 6-8 hours, then drain out the excess juices and shred using two forks.

3 ABSOLUTELY INCREDI-BULL TAKES ON CORN ON THE COB

SERVES: 8-10 * TIME COMMITMENT: 15 MINUTES PREP, 15-20 MINUTES TO COOK

Corn on the cob is fantastic on its own, but gameday calls for a little somethin' somethin'. Thankfully, what makes this veggie over-the-top awesome involves hardly any work, so you can get back to trash-talking the other team in no time.

PARMESAN GARLIC:

1 stick butter
1 tablespoon garlic powder
Shredded Parmesan cheese

CILANTRO LIME:

1 stick butter
4 tablespoons lime juice
3 tablespoons chopped cilantro

HONEY CINNAMON:

1 stick butter
1 1/2 tablespoons honey
1 tablespoon cinnamon

TO MAKE THE FLAVORED BUTTER:

Mix all ingredients in each category and serve atop corn.

TO MAKE THE CORN:

1. Heat the grill on medium. As it warms, peel back the husks without removing them and tear away the silk. Fold the husks back over the corn and submerge in a bowl of ice water. Sprinkle ice water with a tablespoon of salt and a teaspoon of sugar, and let the corn soak for 8-10 minutes.

2. Remove corn from water and shake them off so they're not dripping, then place on the grill and cover it with the lid. Let them cook for 13-15 minutes, turning every 5 minutes or so. It's ready if the kernals feel tender when pierced with a knife.

3. Remove corn from grill, peel off the husks (wear oven mitts or something to protect your hands) and slather with one of these butter combos while they're still warm.

"DODGE THE HURRICANES"
SWEET & SOUR MEATBALL SLIDERS

These sliders are the perfect balance of flavors to describe our regular matchup against Miami: at times delightfully sweet, other times mouth-puckering. Plus, with just four ingredients, they're practically foolproof, so you can keep your focus on the game.

SERVES 5-6   *   TIME COMMITMENT: 5 MINUTES PREP, 2 HOURS COOK TIME

INGREDIENTS:

1 bag frozen beef meatballs

1 (16-ounce) bottle Russian dressing

1 (8-ounce) jar apricot preserves

2 footlong sub rolls

STEPS:

1. Place meatballs, Russian dressing and apricot preserves in a slow cooker. Set to low and let it cook for 2 hours.

2. During the last 5 minutes of cooking, slice open the footlong rolls and lightly butter the inside. Place on a grill or grill pan for 2-3 minutes to lightly toast the bun. Fill the subs with meatballs, and slice into 2-inch servings.

Optional: Hold meatballs in place using toothpicks.

MIKE'S BACON ALFREDO PIZZA

SERVES 8-10 * TIME COMMITMENT: 10 MINUTES PREP, 20 MINUTES TO COOK

In my mind, Mike Wasserman deserves honorary Bull status for this pizza. He may not have attended USF, but his cheesy concoction is the stuff of watch party legend. The key to this no-fail entree is in the dough: Don't buy the cardboard, precooked stuff. You can usually pick up premade dough in your grocery store's bakery or refrigerated foods section, or you can even buy it at a pizzeria for about $2.

INGREDIENTS:

Premade pizza dough

1 cup jarred Alfredo sauce

1 cup shredded mozzarella cheese

6 strips cooked bacon, crumbled

1/2 cup mushrooms, chopped (white/portabella)

STEPS:

1. Preheat the oven to 400° F. Fry bacon until it's crispy and place on a plate lined with paper towels. Let cool, then crumble.

2. Saute the mushrooms in the bacon grease (mushrooms = sponges; they'll absorb some of the bacon flavors).

3. Roll out the dough on a baking sheet lined with parchment paper (or coated with nonstick spray). Apply Alfredo sauce across the whole surface, leaving about 1/2 inch on the sides for crust. Liberally sprinkle cheese across pizza, then the toppings.

4. Cook it in the oven for about 20 minutes or until it's golden brown. Allow it to cool for about 5-7 minutes before devouring.

USF TRIVIA: THE FIRST BOWL GAME WAS IN... (A) 1999, (B) 2003, (C) 2005 OR (D) 2014 IS IT, BABY!

(The answer is on the last page.)

TACO-TONS? WON-TACOS?

SERVES: 8 * TIME COMMITMENT: 30 MINUTES

We love nachos as much as the next person, but the chip-to-toppings ratio is usually wildly off (especially if you invited that nacho hog who seems to always scoop up all of the fillings in the first two bites). These taco wontons ensure the filling-to-crunch ratio is perfect every time.

INGREDIENTS:

1 pound ground beef

1 package taco seasoning

1 can refried beans

1 jalapeño, diced

1 jar fresh salsa

1 package wonton wrappers

1/2 package shredded Mexican cheese

½ cup water

Olive oil (optional)

STEPS:

1. Preheat oven to 350° F. As it preheats, turn a burner to medium heat. Mix ground beef and taco seasoning and cook until beef has fully browned. Drain excess juices and mix seasoned beef with refried beans, chopped jalapeño and 1/2 jar salsa.

2. Place wonton wrappers on a parchment-lined baking sheet. Put one teaspoon taco filling near one corner of each wrapper. Leave about one finger's width between the edge of the wrapper and the filling so you can close the wrapper.

3. Dip your finger into the water and use it to wet the two edges of the wrapper closest to the taco filling. Fold the wrapper in half, so it covers the filling and forms a triangle shape. Use your fingers to seal it, removing any air bubbles.

4. Fold over the two farthest corners of the wrapper, so it forms a small crown, and lightly brush the top of each wonton with olive oil. Place each completed wonton on a baking sheet.

5. Cook wontons for 10-12 minutes, or until lightly browned. Let cool for a few minutes, so they're warm but not hot, and serve with low-sodium soy sauce for dipping.

EXTRA WONTON WRAPPERS? PUT 'EM TO USE WITH THE RECIPE ON PAGE 46.

"DEFEAT THE RED & BLACK" PASTA SALAD

SERVES: 6-8 * TIME COMMITMENT: 10-15 MINUTES PREP, 6-8 MINUTES TO COOK

Game on! This zesty pasta salad storms your tastebuds and means business (kind of like what the Bulls plan on doing to the Cincy Bearcats, right?!). Serve in small tumblers for a single-serving treat: Before filling, dip the rim in water and roll the lip of the cup in a mixture of 2 parts salt and 1 part chili powder, just like you'd salt the rim of a margarita glass.

INGREDIENTS:

1 pound Tri-color Rotini

1 1/4 cups Italian dressing

1/2 red bell pepper

1/2 small vidalia onion

1 cup broccoli florets

1 medium yellow squash

1 medium zucchini

1 cup cauliflower florets

1 can black olives, drained

1/2 pint grape tomatoes, halved

1/2 package matchstick carrots

1/2 hard salami

Crumbled feta

STEPS:

1. Cook rotini according to the package's directions, then strain.
2. Add just enough Italian dressing to the noodles to coat them (about 1 cup) and refrigerate.
3. Chop all veggies and salami to small, bite-sized pieces and add to pasta, mixing in another 1/4 cup of Italian dressing. Chill until ready to serve.

TIP: You can use all of these veggies, or only include the ones you like best. (We like the zucchini-squash-tomato-olive combo to highlight the green and gold Bulls versus the red and black Bearcats, but that's just us.) ♡

59

VEGETABLE MEDLEY FRITTERS

What's been than a veggie platter and a bowl of ranch dip? Veggie fritters and a bowl of ranch dip. These three-bite snacks are flavorful enough on their own, but we'd be lying if we said they weren't even better with a side of everybody's favorite condiment.

SERVES 5-6   *   TIME COMMITMENT: 25 MINUTES

INGREDIENTS:

1 bag frozen vegetable medley (carrots, broccoli, cauliflower)

2 tablespoons water

1 egg

½ cup flour

½ cup shredded parmesan cheese

1 teaspoon minced garlic (or 1 clove, minced)

¼ teaspoon salt

1 teaspoon onion powder (optional)

1-2 tablespoons vegetable oil (or olive, or canola)

STEPS:

1. Place the frozen vegetables in a microwave-safe bowl and add the water. Heat in the microwave for about 10 minutes, or until completely thawed.

2. Chop up the carrot coins into bite-sized pieces, and mash all of the vegetables with the back of a fork so they're about the size of your thumbnail or smaller. (Shortcut: You can also just pulse them in a food processor, if you have one.)

3. Crack an egg into a large mixing bowl and beat it until it's all a pale yellow. Add the flour, cheese, garlic, salt, mashed vegetables and onion powder (if you're including it). Mix everything together to form a paste-like dough.

4. Turn the stovetop to medium-high heat and let the frying pan warm up for about a minute or two. Add the oil and gently swirl the pan so the bottom is coated. Gently drop a few heaping tablespoons of the dough onto the pan, being careful not to let them touch. Let it cook for 2 minutes, then flip and cook for another 1-2 minutes.

5. Set each cooked fritter on a plate lined with paper towels to cool for a few minutes (and collect any excess grease).

"THAT'S ANOTHER FIRST DOWN!" GUACAMOLE

You don't need a reason to chow down on this zesty, tangy, so-good-you'll-eat-it-with-a-spoon guacamole. However, gameday does have its share of rituals, so we'd like to propose one: For every Bulls' first down, treat yourself to a scoop.

SERVES 8-10 * TIME COMMITMENT: 10-12 MINUTES

INGREDIENTS:

2 tablespoons cilantro leaves

½ white onion, finely chopped

1 jalapeño, deseeded and minced

1 teaspoon salt

2 large ripe Haas avocados

1 small plum tomato, diced

1 tablespoon freshly squeezed lime juice

STEPS:

1. Add a spoonful of the cilantro, onion, minced jalapeño and salt in a bowl (a regular old cereal bowl will do) and use the back of a spoon to mash 'em all together.

2. Slice the avocados in half, remove the giant seed in the middle, and use a spoon to scoop out the avocado flesh. (If the avocado's a little brownish in spots, don't worry—it browns like apples do when they're oxidized.) Add the avocado to the bowl and mash it all up until the avocado has formed more of a paste. Some chunks are totally fine!

3. Stir in the rest of the ingredients and serve.

USF TRIVIA:

THE BULLS HAVE THE LARGEST STUDENT SECTION IN THE AMERICAN ATHLETIC CONFERENCE. HOW MANY SEATS DOES IT HOLD?

(A) 12,501   (C) 13,001

(B) 12,001   (D) 13,501

(The answer is on the last page.)

BACON-WRAPPED DATES

SERVES 8

TIME COMMITMENT: 10 MINUTES PREP, 25 MINUTES COOK TIME

Some call these Devils on Horseback (and argue they should be stuffed with almonds -- or mango chutney). We call them delicious. The savory-sweet combination will stun your tastebuds, with or without the devilish additions.

INGREDIENTS:

1 package pitted dates

1 log of goat cheese (any flavor works; 4 ounces)

1 package low-sodium bacon (thick cut if possible)

STEPS:

1. Preheat the oven to 400° F.

2. Slice each date lengthwise, so it opens like a book, and stuff them with goat cheese.

3. Slice each piece of bacon into stubby thirds and wrap a piece around the stuffed date. Place each one on a baking sheet, seam side down. (That way it won't unravel during the cooking process.) Make sure you use a baking sheet with a lip around it, so that bacon grease doesn't drip off the sheet and onto the oven.

4. Bake in the oven for 20-25 minutes, or until the bacon is fully cooked and is no longer translucent.

5. Place dates on a paper towel-lined plate to cool and absorb excess grease.

GUILTLESS VEGGIE FLATBREAD

SERVES: 6-8 * TIME COMMITMENT: 12-14 MINUTES

Variations of this recipe exist all over the web, and while we can't take credit for its invention, we *can* say it tastes incredible. Plus, it balances out all of those fried, saucy tailgate staples.

INGREDIENTS:

1 tube Crescent Rolls
1 8-ounce package cream cheese, softened
1 packet Hidden Valley Ranch dressing mix
Potential toppings:*
Scallions
Grape tomatoes
Broccoli florets
Cauliflower florets
Red peppers
Matchstick carrots

STEPS:

1. Preheat the oven to 375° F. Roll out the crescent dough and pinch the perforated lines to close any holes.

2. Bake for 10 minutes, remove from oven and let cool for 5-7 minutes. In the meantime, combine the cream cheese and ranch dressing mix and spread on the crust. Top with your choice of vegetables and serve chilled.

* Use leftover veggies to make the "Defeat the Red & Black" Pasta Salad!

KNOCK OUT THE "FIGHTIN' IRISH SHEPHERD'S PIE

Some games are so memorable they deserve their own commemorative dish, like when USF upset then-No. 16 Notre Dame in 2011. Even a 43-minute rain delay couldn't drown out the Bulls' drive, and despite a few close calls at the end, they pulled through with a win.

SERVES: 6 * TIME COMMITMENT: 1 HOUR

INGREDIENTS:

1 tube biscuit dough

1 pound ground beef

1/2 onion, finely chopped

1 teaspoon salt

1 tablespoon minced garlic

1 tablespoon flour

1/2 cup beef broth

1 1/2 cups frozen peas and carrots

1 package premade mashed potatoes (about 16 ounces)

2 cups shredded sharp cheddar

STEPS:

1. Preheat the oven to 450° F. As the oven preheats, place one biscuit of dough in each cup of a muffin tin, pressing it down so there's a well for the filling later. Bake the dough for 4-5 minutes, then take it out and set aside.

2. Cook ground beef, salt and garlic in a skillet over medium heat until the beef has browned. Add in the onions, cooking for about 2-3 minutes, or until onions have turned translucent and caramelized.

3. Stir in the flour, then gradually add in the beef broth, peas and carrots. Cook for 2-3 minutes (the flour and broth will form a thin sauce).

4. Fill each biscuit cup halfway with the beef mixture, and top with mashed potatoes. Sprinkle with cheese and cook for 10-12 minutes, or until cheese has melted.

NOTE: THIS RECIPE IS ADAPTED FROM AARON MCCARGO'S RECIPE FOR MINI SHEPHERD'S PIES, WHICH CAN BE FOUND ON FOODNETWORK.COM.

It's not a party without spinach artichoke dip. That's why we're giving you two ways to make it: using an oven *or* microwave.

Ingredients:

2 packages (8 ounces each) reduced fat cream cheese

½ package frozen spinach, thawed and drained

1 can (14 ounces) quartered artichoke hearts, drained

1 teaspoon onion powder

1 teaspoon black pepper

1 teaspoon garlic powder

1¼ cup shredded parmesan cheese

Steps:

1. **Oven Method:** Preheat oven to 450° F. In an oven-safe dish (1.5 quarts or 8-inch x 8-inch works well), combine all ingredients except ¼ cup parmesan cheese. Stir thoroughly.
2. Cook in oven for 12 minutes. Carefully take it out using oven mitts, stir, and sprinkle remaining cheese on top. Turn oven to broil and cook for 4 minutes, or until cheese has melted. Let cool 10-15 minutes before serving.
3. **Microwave Method:** In a microwave-safe dish, combine all ingredients except ¼ cup parmesan cheese, stirring thoroughly. Heat for 4 minutes, stir, then heat for another 4 minutes.
4. Stir in parmesan cheese and cook for 2-3 more minutes, or until the cheeses are mostly melted.

SPINACH ARTICHOKE DIP

SERVES: 4-6   TIME COMMITMENT: 20-ish MINUTES

VEGAN SPINACH ARTICHOKE DIP

SERVES: 6-8

TIME COMMITMENT:
35-40 MINUTES

INGREDIENTS:

1/2 cup mashed red potatoes

2 tablespoons lemon juice

1 tablespoon apple cider vinegar

2 cloves garlic, minced

1 teaspoon salt

1/4 teaspoon freshly ground Black pepper

1 cup soy milk

3 1/2 tablespoons olive oil

1/2 cup bread crumbs

3 tablespoons flat-leaf parsley

1 (14-ounce) can artichoke hearts, drained and rinsed

1/4 cup fresh basil leaves

5 ounces frozen spinach, thawed and drained (1/2 package)

1/4 cup Vegan mozzarella cheese

STEPS:

1. Preheat the oven to 375º F.

2. In a large mixing bowl, add mashed potatoes, lemon juice, vinegar, and garlic, salt, and pepper. Mix it all together until it forms a paste. Add 1/4 cup soy milk and beat on medium until smooth. Add the remaining milk, 3 tablespoonfuls of the oil, and the parsley. Blend until well combined (mixture should be smooth, not chunky), scraping down the sides of the bowl when necessary.

3. Lightly mix in the artichoke, basil and spinach so everything is combined, but it isn't a smooth puree.

4. Pour into a 24- to 36-ounce baking dish.

5. In a separate bowl, combine 1/2 tablespoonful of oil and bread crumbs. Mix well and sprinkle evenly over the dip. Top with vegan cheese.

6. Bake, uncovered, for 25 to 30 minutes.

7. Remove and let cool for about 5 minutes. Stir everything together for a cheesy, melty bowl of goodness.

BAKED SWEET POTATO FRIES WITH HONEY GLAZE

This recipe is a great anytime dish, but it's a nice nod to any North Carolina-based team (ECU, WCU, NCSU, we're lookin' at you), since sweet potatoes are the state dish. If you're tailgating, make a batch beforehand and reheat them on the grill in a foil pouch. You won't regret it.

SERVES: 8-10 * TIME COMMITMENT: 15-20 MINUTES PREP, 10-12 MINUTES TO COOK

INGREDIENTS:

8-9 sweet potatoes

3 1/2 tablespoons honey

2 teaspoons lemon juice

3 tablespoons extra virgin olive oil

2 teaspoons cinnamon

#HowBullsTailgate

Tweet & Instagram using this hashtag & we'll feature your photo on CollegiateCook.com!

STEPS:

1. Preheat the oven to 425° F. While it heats, rinse the potatoes and slice 'em in half horizontally, then cut them into strips about as thick as your pinky finger.

2. In the mixing bowl, combine the honey, cinnamon, lemon juice and olive oil. Once they're thoroughly combined, add in all the sweet potato slices, tossing them so they're lightly glazed in the sauce. (Even if it looks like they're barely coated, trust me — the flavor will be there. If they're dripping before they bake, they'll turn out mushy. Still delicious, but not very fry-like.)

3. Place the potatoes on a baking sheet. It's okay if they touch.

4. Bake in the oven for 10-12 minutes, or until lightly browned. Some of the edges may blacken, but never fear — that's a sign of deliciousness. Just don't let the entire fry get that way.

READY-FOR-KICKOFF SLOW COOKER CHILI

SERVES: 6   *   TIME COMMITMENT: 6 HOURS

There's no better way to get ready for kickoff on a chilly December night than with a proper chili cookoff, and this recipe is your secret weapon. Serve with Cavatappi pasta and shredded cheese for a truly incredible dish.

INGREDIENTS:

1½ pounds ground beef or ground turkey

1 large green bell pepper

1 medium onion

1 can pinto beans (16 ounces)

1 can black-eyed peas (16 ounces)

1 can tomato sauce (8 ounces)

1 envelope chili seasoning

2 cloves garlic, minced

1 package Cavatappi, Rigatoni or Elbow Macaroni, cooked

Shredded cheddar or Gouda cheese, optional

STEPS:

1. Brown the ground beef (or ground turkey) in a saute pan over medium heat until it's fully cooked and no longer pink. Drain any excess juices and set aside.

2. Chop the green pepper and onion, and pour into the slow cooker. Add in the ground beef, beans, tomato sauce, chili seasoning and garlic. Cook over low heat for 6-8 hours, or until ingredients are warmed.

3. Serve atop cooked pasta, and sprinkle with cheese if you'd like.

POPCORN SHRIMP MINI-SUBS

Consider it the world's easiest twist on a Po'Boy: all you need is a few minutes and a few ingredients, and you've got a main course that's worthy of its own halftime show. Who knew crisp coleslaw was such a great complement to popcorn shrimp?

SERVES: 4-6   *   TIME COMMITMENT: 20-25 MINUTES

INGREDIENTS:

Frozen popcorn shrimp

1 bag coleslaw mix (find in the produce section, near the bagged salads)

3 tablespoons mayonnaise

1 tablespoon garlic powder

1 teaspoon cayenne pepper

1/4 teaspoon salt

Hoagie/sub rolls

STEPS:

1. Cook frozen shrimp according to the package's instructions. (So far, so easy, right?) Set aside.

2. In a separate bowl, combine 2 cups of the coleslaw mix with mayonnaise, garlic powder, cayenne pepper and salt. Sample and adjust seasonings to your taste.

3. Slather a footlong sub roll with as much slaw as you like, line with popcorn shrimp, and cut into 3-inch sections.

USF TRIVIA: THE MEDIA WENT CRAZY WHEN COACH TAGGART WORE WHAT SHIRT TO PRACTICE IN 2013?

(Answer on last page.)

BACON RANCH SHREDDED CHICKEN

SERVES: 5   *   TIME COMMITMENT: 8 HOURS

Bacon. Ranch. Shredded chicken. It's so many things. All of which are delicious. This slow cooker recipe basically cooks itself, and can be served on rolls for a new take on tailgate sliders, or mixed with pasta for a team dinner that satisfies even the heartiest of appetites.

INGREDIENTS:

5 slices of bacon

2 cloves minced garlic

1 can reduced-sodium cream of chicken soup (10.75 ounces)

1 cup sour cream

½ cup water

½ teaspoon pepper

1½ pounds boneless, skinless chicken breasts

1 package Cavatappi pasta

1 bundle chives, chopped

STEPS:

1. Chop the bacon and cook in a frying pan until it's no longer translucent but not totally crispy. Set on a plate lined with paper towels to drain off excess grease.

2. In a mixing bowl, combine garlic, cream of chicken soup, sour cream, water and pepper. Add in bacon, stirring to combine everything, then add in the chicken breasts, so they're coated in the mixture. Pour everything into the slow cooker, and place on low heat for 6-8 hours.

3. Once it's ready, use two forks to shred the chicken. Serve the chicken and sauce atop the pasta, and garnish with chives.

USF TRIVIA: THE CITY OF TAMPA RECOGNIZES WHICH DATE AS USF DAY?

(Answer on last page.)

CHOCOLATE-HAZELNUT
COWBOY COOKIES,
PAGE 98

SWEET TREATS

NO WATCH PARTY IS COMPLETE WITHOUT A JOLT OF SUGAR. TRUST US.

Scan to shop for Green & Gold
M&Ms and other gameday
essentials at CollegiateCook.com!

ROCKY'S UNSTOPPABULL SNACK MIX

The best part about this mix? You can make it your own! If you're not a fan of peanut butter, you can coat the Chex with an equal amount of melted white or dark chocolate, or butter mixed with a teaspoon of cinnamon.

SERVES 4-6

INGREDIENTS:

½ cup peanut butter chips

1 teaspoon canola oil

4 cups Honey Nut Chex

2 cups pretzels

1 cup green and yellow M&Ms

2 cups popcorn

1 cup pistachios

STEPS:

1. Place peanut butter chips and canola oil in a bowl and microwave for 20 seconds. Stir & continue heating in 20-second intervals until melted.

2. Toss the Chex and melted peanut butter in a large mixing bowl until the cereal is lightly coated. Line a baking sheet with parchment paper and spread a thin layer of cereal across it. Put it in the fridge to set for 5-7 minutes.

3. Break up the coated Chex into bite-sized pieces, then toss in a mixing bowl with the other ingredients.

"THAT'S BS!" COOKIES
(AKA 'GREEN & GOLDIES' AKA 'COWPIE COOKIES')

If you've ever attended a USF football game, you may have noticed people have a common catchphrase they like to shout when they feel the ref has made a bad call. (Let's just say it rhymes with bullspit, and it comes with a graphic gesture.) This take on the classic cowpie cookie winks at the old phrase, and is perfect for those moments when you need to stuff your face to keep from hurling expletives.

YIELDS 2 DOZEN COOKIES   *   TIME COMMITMENT: 10 MINUTES TO PREP, 9-11 MINUTES COOK TIME

INGREDIENTS:

1 stick unsalted butter, softened

3/4 cup granulated sugar

1/2 cup brown sugar

1 egg

1 teaspoon vanilla extract

3/4 cup flour

1/4 cup cocoa powder

1/4 teaspoon salt

1/2 teaspoon baking soda

1 1/2 cups quick-cooking oats

1 cup peanut butter chips

1 bag mint M&Ms, crushed

STEPS:

1. Preheat the oven to 350° F. As it heats, beat the butter, granulated sugar and brown sugar in a large bowl until it's light and fluffy (about two minutes). Blend in the egg and vanilla.

2. In another bowl, combine the flour, cocoa, baking soda and salt, then gradually stir in the butter/sugar mixture and the oats. Once those are all mixed together, fold in the peanut butter chips and crushed M&Ms.

3. Use a teaspoon to dole out one-inch blobs of dough and place them on the cookie sheet, about 1 1/2 inches apart. Bake for 9-11 minutes, or until edges have set and the center still appears moist.
(It will finish cooking as it cools.)

"SWEET VICTORY" / "DROWN YOUR SORROWS"
BOOZY GREEN VELVET CUPCAKES

If you win, enjoy a cupcake. If you lose...enjoy two? These green velvet mini-cakes are topped with a swirl of vodka-spiked cream cheese frosting, making them a fun alternative to those cliched Jell-o shots (or just plain ol' shots-shots). Change the food coloring to match your team's — or opponent's — colors, and you can sub in any kind of alcohol you choose if vodka's not your thing.

SERVES 30 MINI CUPCAKES ✱ TIME COMMITMENT: 20 MINUTES PREP, 10-12 MINUTES TO COOK

GREEN VELVET CAKE INGREDIENTS:

1 egg
1/2 cup oil (vegetable or canola)
1/2 cup buttermilk
1 1/4 cups flour
1 cup sugar
1/2 teaspoon salt
1 1/2 teaspoons cocoa powder
1 teaspoon vanilla extract
1 1/2-2 teaspoons food coloring
1/2 teaspoon baking soda
1 1/2 tablespoons vinegar

BOOZY FROSTING INGREDIENTS:

2 tablespoons unsalted butter, softened
3 ounces cream cheese
3 cups powdered sugar
1/4 cup marshmallow or whipped cream-flavored vodka

STEPS:

1. **For the cake:** Beat eggs, oil and buttermilk

2. In a separate bowl, combine flour, sugar and salt. Gradually blend this into the liquid mixture, using an electric mixer on low-to-medium speed (or some good ol' fashioned whisk-and-bicep action).

3. In the now-empty dry ingredients bowl (or a third small bowl), mix the cocoa powder, vanilla and food coloring until it forms a gel-like paste. Scrape it out and blend it into the cake batter.

4. Grab that once-again-empty dry ingredients bowl and pour in the baking soda and vinegar. Stir, and as it bubbles up, pour the mixture into the batter. Stir the batter just enough to combine the fizzy vinegar. Pour the batter into mini cupcake tins, filling each one 2/3s of the way.

5. **For the frosting:** Blend the butter, cream cheese and powdered sugar until it's light and fluffy. Beat at a low speed as you slowly pour in the vodka (think of it like a slow, steady stream, so you don't wind up with a frosting puddle), and blend until it's fully combined.

6. Pour frosting into a piping bag or a plastic resealable bag (snip a corner to create a spout), and swirl the frosting onto each cooled cupcake.

Note: For an alcohol-free version, cut out the vodka and reduce powdered sugar to 2 cups.

> ### DISCLAIMER:
> These treats are for those over 21, since the alcohol doesn't bake off.
> Please eat responsibly.

CHOCOLATE & PEANUT BUTTER-DRIZZLED POPCORN

Here's a delicious twist on a classic gameday favorite that is guaranteed to get the crowd out of their seats and huddled around this dish. Popcorn + Chocolate + Peanut Butter. Now that's an all-star team!

Serves: 6   *   TIME COMMITMENT: 10 MINUTES

INGREDIENTS:

1 bag popcorn

1 cup semisweet chocolate chips

1 tablespoon butter

3 tablespoons peanut butter

Sprinkle sea salt (optional)

STEPS:

1. Microwave popcorn according to the package instructions, and pour across a baking sheet lined with parchment paper.

2. Place chocolate chips and butter in a microwave-safe bowl. Microwave for 20 seconds, stir, and repeat process until chips are melted. Do the same with the peanut butter. Drizzle both atop the popcorn and top with a light sprinkling of sea salt.

"SPEAR THOSE KNIGHTS"
FRUIT KABOBS WITH HONEY CARAMEL SAUCE

They call it the "War on I-4" for a reason: UCF and USF are bitter rivals, but there's nothing sour about this snack. Sprinkle a little coarse sea salt on top of the caramel dip to intensify the flavor (perfect when things start getting tense in the second half).

Warning: The caramel sauce will bubble and can burn you if it splatters on you. Please be careful and use a long spatula and keep your hair back while cooking.

SERVES 5-6 * TIME COMMITMENT: 10 MINUTES TO PREP, 8-9 MINUTES COOK TIME

INGREDIENTS:

1 cup buttermilk
¾ cup sugar
½ stick unsalted butter
1 tablespoon honey
½ teaspoon baking soda
½ teaspoon salt
1 teaspoon vanilla extract
4 apples
4 bananas
½ cup lemon juice

STEPS:

1. **First, the sauce:** Combine buttermilk, sugar, butter, honey, baking soda & salt into a large saucepan. (The mixture will bubble up to about twice its size during the cooking process, so the larger the pan, the better.) Place the saucepan on a burner turned to medium-high, and stir as it starts to bubble.

2. Bring the mixture to a boil, stirring frequently, and as soon as it starts to boil, reduce the heat to medium and bring it to a light simmer (it should still bubble a bit). Set a timer for 8 minutes and put those arms to work stirring almost nonstop.

3. Once the time is up, remove from heat and stir in the vanilla. The caramel should be a dark golden brown color. The bubbles will slowly disappear as it sits for a few minutes. Give it 15-20 minutes to cool before serving.

4. While the sauce cools, slice the bananas and cube the apples. Toss both in lemon juice to keep them from oxidizing and turning brown, then slide them onto toothpicks or skewers.

Tip: If the sauce hardens, place it in the microwave for 20-30 seconds, give it a good stir, and repeat until it reaches your desired consistency.

DANIELLE'S GLUTEN-FREE
CHOCOLATE CHIP COOKIES

Forget an apple a day — any doctor who recommends cookies becomes my go-to M.D. Okay, so maybe USF alum Dr. Danielle Kurant didn't actually *say* cookies are a healthy part of every diet, but she did give me this can't-believe-it's-gluten-free recipe. (Not crazy about bananas? Don't worry; you can't taste 'em!)

SERVINGS: YIELDS 1 DOZEN COOKIES   *   TIME COMMITMENT: 15-17 MINUTES

INGREDIENTS:

1 medium banana

1 egg

1 cup peanut butter

1/2 teaspoon baking soda

1/2 cup sugar

A pinch of salt

1 1/2 cups semisweet chocolate chips

STEPS:

1. Preheat your oven to 350° F.
2. Mash up the banana as finely as possible (opt for one that's beginning to brown — it'll naturally sweeten the cookies) and place it in a mixing bowl.
3. Add in the egg, peanut butter, baking soda, sugar, salt and mix thoroughly. Fold in the chocolate chips.
4. Spoon cookies onto a baking sheet, placing them about an inch apart.
5. Bake for 10-12 minutes, or until the cookies are lightly golden brown. Let them cool for a few minutes before serving.

UH, WHAT ARE THOSE WHITE, STRINGY BITS IN MY EGG?

They're the chalazae, and while they're completely harmless, they don't break down during the cooking process, so you can bite into a hardened bit. Most chefs say they're only noticeable in custards and puddings, but I usually remove them from desserts.

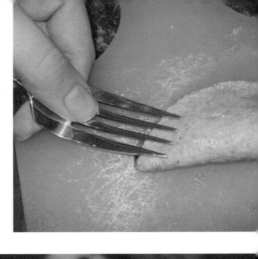
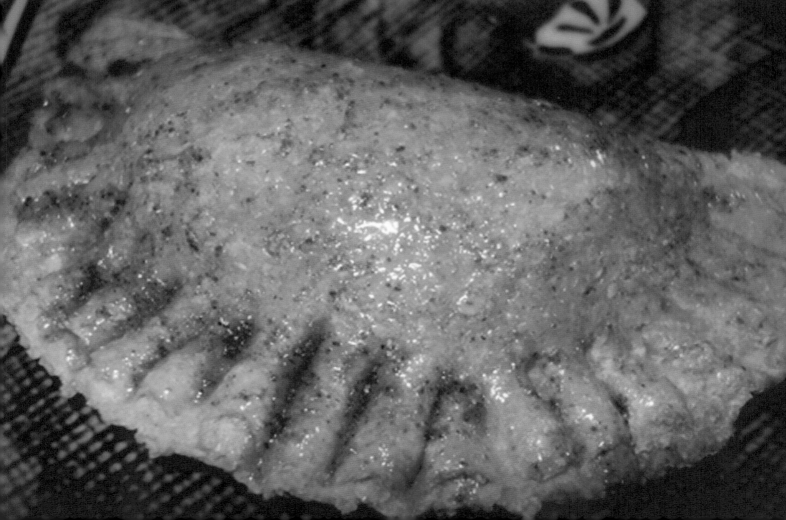

BAKED APPLE EMPANADAS

Considering these empanadas' oval-like shape, it may be tempting to play tabletop football with these sweets (subbing in your mouth for the goalposts, of course), but trust us, you wouldn't want to risk a wayward empanada falling to the ground. They're just too good to waste. (Also, no rolling pin? No problem -- try a can wrapped in plastic wrap.)

YIELDS 16 PIES   TAKES 40-45 MINUTES

INGREDIENTS:

Dough:
3 cups flour
2 egg yolks, beaten
2 tablespoons sugar
1/2 cup water
1/4 teaspoon salt

Filling:
3-4 apples (gala are great)
1 cup granulated sugar
1 tablespoon cinnamon
1/2 teaspoon nutmeg

STEPS:

1. Preheat the oven to 350° F. In a large mixing bowl, beat the egg yolks using a folk, then mix in the water, salt and sugar. Add in the flour, kneading everything together with your hands.

2. Let dough sit for 10-12 minutes. Peel, core and dice the apples.

3. Place the chopped apples into a saucepan, adding in the sugar, cinnamon and nutmeg. Cook on medium heat, stirring continually, for about 7-9 minutes, or until the apples are soft/slightly translucent.

4. Place the apples in the fridge to cool. Roll out the dough as thin as you can get it (1/8" or less). *If you don't have a rolling pin, use a soda can wrapped in a resealable bag.*

5. Cut the dough into 4-inch circles. *If you don't have a cookie cutter, place a cup face down and trace around it with a knife.*

6. Take out the apple filling and place about a teaspoon to a tablespoon's worth on each disc of dough. Leave 1/2 an inch uncovered on all sides so the filling will be less likely to seep out.

7. Flip the dough in half, creating a semi-circle. Use a fork to press down on the edges of the semi-circle, crimping it closed.

8. Use the excess juices from the apple filling to lightly coat the tops of the empanadas. Place the empanadas in the oven for 14-16 minutes, or until the crust has become a light golden brown.

Fourth-Quarter KABOOM! Cookies

We all crave those moments when we're down by 3 with just minutes left in the game, when suddenly a running back shoots off like a rocket, zipping down the field for a TOUCHDOOOOOWN! The crowd explodes with excitement, just like these sugar cookies explode with the crackling delight that is Pop Rocks.

Serves 7-8　　✳　　TIME COMMITMENT: 20 minutes to prep, 10-11 minutes to cook, 20-25 minutes to decorate

INGREDIENTS:

Dough:
  1 cup shortening
  1 cup butter, softened
  1 cup sugar
  1 egg
  1 teaspoon vanilla extract
  1 ¾ cups flour
  1 teaspoon baking powder
  ¾ teaspoon salt

"Exploding" Center & Decorations:
  3 packages of Pop Rocks

  Optional, but great for decorating Rainbow sprinkles, M&Ms Minis, mini chocolate chips, Red Hots, Sno Caps, crushed peanut butter cups

Cream Cheese Frosting:
  3 ounces of cream cheese

  2 tablespoons unsalted butter, softened

  2 cups powdered sugar

STEPS:

1. Preheat the oven to 350° F. As it heats, cream the butter, shortening and sugar until it's light and fluffy. Mix in the egg and vanilla extract.

2. In a separate bowl, combine the flour, baking soda and salt. Gradually mix this into the butter/sugar concoction until it forms a lighter-than-Play-Doh dough.

3. For a tie-dye effect, set aside half of the dough and mix 4-6 drops of food coloring into it. Twist the two balls of dough together — just about 4 or 5 times — to create swirls of color in it. (Too much twisting will turn the whole thing a dull gray.)

4. Tape a piece of parchment paper to a table, lightly flour it and your rolling pin, and roll out your dough. Press lightly — this dough can crumble easily — and move the rolling pin in different directions to keep the dough from tearing. Once it's about ¼-inch thick, take cookie cutters and cut out whatever shapes you desire, then transfer them to a parchment paper-lined baking sheet.

5. It takes 3 cookies to make each exploding cookie. Use a knife to cut a hole in 1 out of every 3 — that will be the middle cookie, which stores the candy. It's best to cut the holes once they're already on the baking sheet, so you don't have to move them (and risk tearing the cookie).

6. Bake 10-11 minutes. Let cool fully (about 20 minutes) before decorating. Turn off the oven.

7. Blend all frosting ingredients together on medium speed until a thick, paste-like frosting appears. (If yours looks too runny, add a tablespoon or two of powdered sugar and blend.) Frost the top and bottom of the cookie with a hole in it. Stick it atop one whole cookie, pour in the Pop Rocks (or whatever candy you chose) and top with another whole cookie. Press the cookie edges lightly to seal.

8. Bedazzle as you see fit! I like to coat the edges with frosting and roll the cookies in sprinkles or crushed candy.

CHOCOLATE-HAZELNUT COWBOY COOKIES

These cookies originated in Colorado, but we say they're a fitting dessert when the Bulls are up against the McNeese State Cowboys. Then again, we're a bit biased: We love this riff on the classic oatmeal cookie so much we want it on hand at *every* tailgate.

SERVINGS: YIELDS 2 DOZEN COOKIES ✱ TIME COMMITMENT: 10 MINUTES PREP, 10-12 MINUTES TO COOK

INGREDIENTS:

1 stick unsalted butter, softened
1/2 cup packed brown sugar
1/3 cup granulated sugar
1 egg, room temperature
1 teaspoon vanilla extract
1 cup rolled oats
1 cup flour
1/2 teaspoon baking soda
1/4 teaspoon baking powder
1/4 teaspoon salt
1/4 teaspoon cinnamon
1 cup semisweet chocolate chips
1/2 cup chopped hazelnuts

STEPS:

1. Preheat the oven to 350° F. Next, beat the butter and sugars using an electric mixer (or whisk your way to Michelle Obama arms) until they're almost the color and texture of hummus. Add in the eggs and vanilla extract, beating at a medium speed until the mixture is smooth and almost frosting-like in consistency.

2. In another bowl, stir together the next six ingredients: oats, flour, baking soda, baking powder, salt and cinnamon. Gradually mix this into the butter/egg/sugar concoction. Fold in the chocolate chips and hazelnuts.

3. Use a teaspoon to dish out roughly one-inch balls of dough, and place them about 1 ½ inches apart on the cookie sheet. Bake for 10-12 minutes, or until lightly golden. The center should still look a little moist; it will finish baking as it cools.

FRUIT SALSA WITH BAKED CINNAMON CHIPS

Now this is feel-good tailgate food. You can use any combination of fruit you'd like, though we highly recommend keeping the lemon juice — not only does it balance out the sweetness of the fruit, it keeps them from browning, so your dish earns "ooohs," not "ewws."

SERVES: 8-10 ＊ TIME COMMITMENT: 7-9 MINUTES PREP, 5-6 MINUTES TO COOK

INGREDIENTS:

For the chips:

10 (8-inch) flour tortillas

1 can spray canola oil

1/2 cup sugar

2 tablespoons cinnamon

For the fruit salsa:

1/2 can crushed pineapple

2/3 can mandarin oranges

1 Granny Smith apple

8-10 strawberries

1 tablespoon lemon juice

STEPS:

For the chips:

1. Preheat the oven to 350° F. As it heats, combine the sugar and cinnamon.

2. Next, place tortillas on the baking sheet(s). Lightly mist them with spray oil (or brush them with a paper towel dipped in canola oil, if you don't have the spray kind), and sprinkle on cinnamon sugar.

3. Slice the tortillas into wedges and let them cook for about 5-6 minutes, or until they're lightly golden. Repeat the baking process as necessary until all of the chips have been made.

For the fruit salsa:

4. Drain excess juice from the pineapples and oranges.

5. Wash the rest of the fruit, then finely chop all of it. (Or pulse it into the food processor, if you're schfancy like that.)

6. Add all of the fruit into a serving dish and mix it with a tablespoon of lemon juice. Serve chilled.

CHOCOLATE-COVERED FROZEN BANANAS

If you're hosting a watch party, we highly recommend a frozen banana bar. Fill a fondue pot with chocolate, line up bowls of any toppings that interest you, and watch people lose their minds over this guilt-free dessert.

Serves: 6 * TIME COMMITMENT: 15 MINUTES

INGREDIENTS:

1 cup semisweet chocolate chips

1 tablespoon butter

3 bananas, cut in half

Crushed candies, nuts or other toppings of your choice

Toppings We Love:

Cereal, peanuts, melted peanut butter, crumbled candy bars, cookie bits, M&Ms, dried cranberries

STEPS:

1. Insert a straw (or popsicle stick or whatever you're using) halfway into the banana. Place bananas on a plate or baking sheet and freeze for one hour.

2. Place chocolate chips and shortening in a microwave-safe bowl and heat for 30-second intervals, stirring in between, until they're completely melted. This should take about a minute and a half.

3. Hold the banana-stick over the bowl of chocolate sauce and use a spoon to drizzle the chocolate on the banana to coat it. *(**Note:** Dipping the banana into the bowl of chocolate sauce just causes the sauce to harden quickly.)*

4. As soon as the banana's coated, roll it in the ingredients of your choice, then set it on a plate or baking sheet to harden.

USF TRIVIA: THE "GO BULLS" HAND SIGN STARTED AS A GOOD LUCK SYMBOL. IN WHICH SITUATION(S) DID PEOPLE ORIGINALLY PUT UP THE HORNS, AND FOR WHAT SPORT?

(Answer on last page.)

NO-BAKE TRUFFLES

These treats are completely customizable: just about any cookie will do (in fact, they're a great way to use up old ones!) and you can dip them, fondue-style, in just about anything. Maybe not cheese. Yeah, definitely not cheese.

SERVINGS: YIELDS 3 DOZEN TRUFFLES   *   TIME COMMITMENT: 20-25 MINUTES

CHOCOLATE CHIP TRUFFLE INGREDIENTS:

- 13oz box crispy chocolate chip cookies
- 1 (8-ounce) tub of cream cheese
- 1 cup semisweet chocolate chips
- 2 tbsp of oil: canola or vegetable

OREO AND WHITE CHOCOLATE TRUFFLE INGREDIENTS:

- 14.3oz box Oreos chocolate cookies
- 1 (8-ounce) tub of cream cheese
- 1 cup white chocolate chips
- 2 tbsp of oil: canola or vegetable

TEDDY GRAHAMS TRUFFLE INGREDIENTS:

- 10oz box honey Teddy Grahams
- 1/2 tub of cream cheese
- 1/2 peanut butter
- 1 cup semisweet chocolate chips
- 2 tbsp of oil: canola or vegetable

STEPS:

1. Place a few cookies in a resealable bag. Then, using a spoon, smash those cookies to smithereens. Repeat until all are smashed.

2. Pour cookie bits in a bowl & mix in cream cheese (& peanut butter, if making the Teddy Grahams version) until a dough forms. Roll into 1-inch balls & place on baking sheet.

3. Place them in the freezer for 15-20 minutes to harden.

4. Add oil and chips into a microwave-safe bowl and microwave in 20-second intervals until fully melted, stirring between each interval.

5. Using a toothpick, dip each ball into the melted chocolate sauce and coat completely. Place each back on the baking sheet, then return truffles to the freezer for 15 minutes to harden the coating.

Optional: Prior to returning truffles to the freezer to harden, dust each ball with additional crumbled cookie.

105

A TASTE OF
GAMEDAY

A LOOK INSIDE FOOTBALL CULTURE AT USF * #HOWBULLSTAILGATE

THE ULTIMATE TAILGATE MACHINE

WHEN THE USF SOCIETY OF AUTOMOTIVE ENGINEERS ISN'T DESIGNING, BUILDING AND RACING FORMULA 1-STYLE RACECARS, THE ORGANIZATION IS DOMINATING THE TAILGATING SCENE. PR OFFICER JACQUELINE LEBRUN TAKES US INSIDE THE BUS:

What's a tailgate like with SAE?
Tailgating with SAE is always fun. We bring the bus, along with all the tailgate essentials: BBQ, cold drinks, games and school spirit! When we worked with alumni and our former sponsor NOS Energy Drinks, we would set up massive displays with DJs and video game systems. Even without all the fun extras, being able to hang out with the team and relax for an afternoon is enjoyable.

What are some of the bus's special features? (We heard you tow a Jacuzzi?!)
The bus has a ton of extra features since we use it as an RV during our competition season. Inside we have bunk beds, tables and bench seats, a refrigerator and freezer, an awesome sound system, as well as a stove range and sink for tailgate food prep! One of our alumni would bring the Jacuzzi for us. We'd haul barrels of water and tow the Jacuzzi from USF to the tailgate site so we can hang out and take a dip to avoid the blistering Florida sun.

Do you have any gameday rituals?
When we can, we park next to the crosswalk where fans head to the stadium. We try to get them as pumped up as possible by cheering and starting chants.

LEARN MORE ABOUT USF SAE BY VISTING USFRACING.COM OR FOLLOWING @USFSAE ON TWITTER!

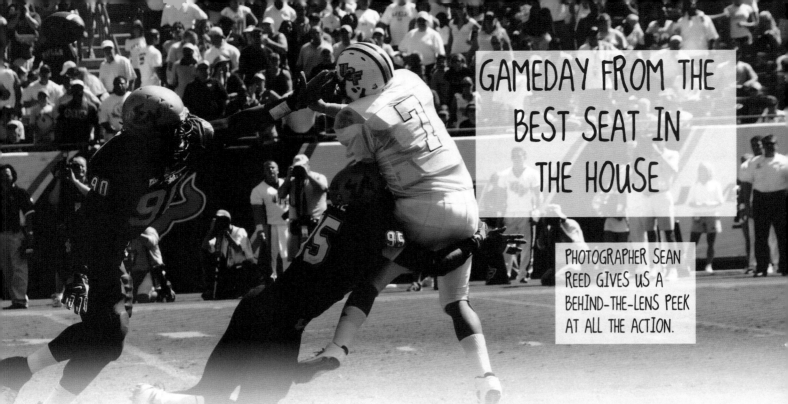

GAMEDAY FROM THE BEST SEAT IN THE HOUSE

PHOTOGRAPHER SEAN REED GIVES US A BEHIND-THE-LENS PEEK AT ALL THE ACTION.

How do you prep for a game?

I tried to do a little pre-game research. The sports editor would usually have some specific players in mind for the game — someone who's been noteworthy at practices, for example. I also checked out the other team's players. The big-name players would generally be where the action is on the field, so it was good to know ahead of time so I could anticipate some shots.

What's it like on the field?

It's a cool experience. The most memorable game was when USF played West Virginia (in 2007, I think). The crowd was huge, and they were loud. When they would really get going, it made the hair on the back of my neck stand up. You just kind of look around and realize you're surrounded by a sea of jumping, screaming people.

Is there anything people wouldn't expect about shooting a USF football game?

There is a LOT of running. Before I got to the first game, I expected a little movement, but figured there would be enough downtime between plays to get things situated. I got my first dose of reality when there was a long pass, and the players were now at the other end of the field, and I had to get there quickly!

What advice would you give to anyone interested in sports photography?

Volunteer for any sports-related opportunities you can find. Some sports are less entertaining than others, but they all helped me develop different skills.

From a logistics standpoint: Show up early. Get a feel for the lighting. Find out where you'll be allowed to shoot from.

THE LIFE OF THE PARTY: BEEF STUDS & BEEF BABES

COURTNEY LEINEKE & JERRY TROTTER TELL US WHAT IT'S LIKE TO BE PART OF ONE OF THE MOST SPIRITED GROUPS ON CAMPUS.

How long does it take to get painted up, and how early do the Beef Studs tend to show up before games?

Courtney: It usually takes around 5-10 minutes, depending on the painter and the person. A whole group before a game takes hours. We usually show up when the gates open, which is about five hours prior to game time.

What's the best part of being a Beef Stud?

Jerry: Family and energy. Studs were always there for each other — I made some pretty great friendships from my tenure, and equally great memories. And, there is one thing I can say was always true about them — they bring the energy.

What was your most memorable experience as a Beef Stud?

Jerry: One of my favorite memories was the road trip to El Paso and attending that year's bowl game. A fellow stud and I had so much fun revving up the crowd that we wondered into the opposing teams' student section and started cheering there. Fans on both sides were such great sports. Although the Oregon Duck band director did not take too kindly to my attempts at orchestrating the band.

What advice would you have for anyone who's considering becoming a Beef Stud or Beef Babe?

Courtney: You have to try it at least once! Let everything go. Don't worry about your body type or the way you look, or if you're acting weird. It's an experience you'll be able to talk about forever.

WHAT TAILGATING'S LIKE WHEN YOU'RE 1,000 MILES AWAY
CASSIE HANJIAN SHOWS US HOW SHE (AND OTHER ALUMNI) CELEBRATE FOOTBALL SEASON IN NEW YORK CITY

What goes into planning a USF Alumni Association Watch Party?

Watch Party planning can be a little like juggling: there are a lot of moving parts that you have to be aware of at all times. You have to make sure you find a good location — one that's centrally located for the majority of the alumni in your area and is flexible with what can often be an unpredictable season schedule. Outside of Florida, it's much harder to ensure that the game will be shown in your location, so it's important to keep apprised of the broadcast channel.

There's also a lot of brainstorming: we consider which gameday specials will attract our members, what to give away for raffle prizes each week and what other activities we can incorporate to keep alumni interested and involved.

What was the process like for creating those specialty drinks? Which one was your favorite?

When I first started serving on the alumni association board, I wanted to create something that would be distinct and interesting for each game. For the past two seasons, we had a different cocktail each week that related to the opposing team's mascot. (For example, when we played Miami, we had hurricanes.)

This year we're going to do one specialty "Bulls" drink for the whole season that will be voted on by our members. My favorite drink was the specialty cocktail we had for the Notre Dame game: Irish Eyes, which tasted like mint chocolate chip ice cream. Yum!

Right now, I'm doing a slow motion-victory dance (horribly out of rhythm, I assure you) just for the very fact that you've picked up this book. Seriously, THANK YOU.

It means so much to me that you took the time to pick up *Collegiate Cook's USF Gameday Recipes*. I am so grateful, and I hope you've enjoyed the recipes.

This book wouldn't be possible if it weren't for my incredible husband, Nathan. He took most of the photos, even in the midst of a heatwave in our cramped, A/C-less kitchen, as we fought with a barely functioning extension cord that made our lights short out roughly every 36 seconds. He also helped design the book.

Also, huge, tremendous all-caps THANKS to my Mom and Dad for helping test recipes (endlessly) as we tweaked everything to get it just right, and taking recipe shots along the way! My mom was the tireless engineer behind the Shrimp Mini Subs, Sweet & Sour Meatball Sliders, Red & Black Pasta Salad and Houston, Texas Margaritas.

Also, Cynthia Roldan, Sean Reed and Matt Congrove, thank you for taking such phenomenal photos at games and tailgates, and for being all-around awesome people. You rock. For reals.

Lastly, my unending gratitude to the folks who dreamed up (and fight for) Bright Futures, the USF donors, Florida Swimming Pool Association, Jim Bertelsmeyer, Lyle Blanden, the National Propane Gas Association and all of the other incredibly generous souls who contributed to my college education, providing the funding for the various scholarships that allowed me to graduate debt-free. I am so glad to be able to pay it forward in a small way with this cookbook. Hopefully more to come.

Coach T, thanks for driving the bus!

—Candace

BUT WAIT, THERE'S MORE! FOR ADDITIONAL RECIPES & TAILGATE IDEAS, VISIT COLLEGIATECOOK.COM

INDEX

THE USF TRIVIA ANSWERS YOU'VE BEEN DYING FOR:

Page 13: C. 29 degrees, in a game against WVU in 2008

Page 15: B. Concurrent Kicks; This is a tricky one. The Sun Dolls do concurrent kicks while the cheerleaders do pushups.

Page 27: John S. Allen

Page 35: The Bulls played the Florida Gators and won 85-78.

Page 39: HOT debuted in 1999.

Page 45: A. Desert Rats (Other names considered were the Buccaneers and Florida Chickens.)

Page 55: C. 2005; The Bulls played NC State in the Meineke Car Care Bowl

Page 63: A. 12,501

Page 77: Coach Taggart wore a blue buttondown with a "Willie" nametag, which symbolized the blue-collar work ethic.

Page 79: April 9

Page 103: It was used during free-throw shots in basketball.

PHOTOS COURTESY OF...

Nathan Davison
Matt Congrove
Sean Reed
Cynthia Roldan
Melodene & Gary Braun
Cassie Hanjian
Greg & Megan Morgan
USF SAE
Michelle Joy
Amanda Wintenburg
Courtney Leineke
Jerry Trotter
Sean & Meagan Phillips
Michelle Husselman

38490022R00066

Made in the USA
Charleston, SC
06 February 2015